HEALING
DEVOTIONAL

HEALING DEVOTIONAL

Encountering Your Path to Healing

DR. KEVIN L. ZADAI

Cover design: Virtually Possible Designs
For more information about our school, go to
www.warriornotesschool.com. Reach us on the internet:
www.Kevinzadai.com

ISBN 13 TP: 978-1-6631-0001-6

Dedication

I dedicate this book to the Lord Jesus Christ. When I died during surgery and met with Jesus on the other side, He insisted that I return to life on the earth and that I help people with their destinies. Because of Jesus' love and concern for people, the Lord has actually chosen to send a person back from death to help everyone who will receive that help so that his or her destiny and purpose are secure in Him. I want You, Lord, to know that when You come to take me to be with You someday, it is my sincere hope that people remember not me, but the revelation of Jesus Christ that You have revealed through me. I want others to know that I am merely being obedient to Your Heavenly calling and mission, which is to reveal Your plan for the fulfillment of the divine destiny for each of God's children.

Acknowledgments

In addition to sharing my story with everyone through the book *Heavenly Visitation: A Guide to the Supernatural,* God has commissioned me to write over fifty books and study guides. Most recently, the Lord gave me the commission to produce this *Healing Devotional.* This daily devotional addresses some of the revelations concerning the areas that Jesus reviewed and revealed to me through the Word of God and by the Spirit of God during several visitations. I want to thank everyone who has encouraged me, assisted me, and prayed for me during the writing of this work, especially my spiritual parents, Dr. Jesse Duplantis and Dr. Cathy Duplantis. Special thanks to my wonderful wife Kathi for her love and dedication to the Lord and me. Thank you to a great staff for the wonderful job editing this book. Special thanks, as well, to all my friends who know about *Healing* and how to operate in this for the next move of God's Spirit!

CONTENTS

INTRODUCTION

In this 60-day Healing Devotional, I am going to show you that God's will is for us to be well. As Christians, it is part of our inheritance. Jesus healed all who were oppressed by the devil, and He said that we would do greater works! Through this devotional you will learn how to pray for yourself to receive healing, how to pray for others to receive healing, the authority of the believer, how Jesus administered healing, the devil's role in sickness, how God's goodness causes people to be healed even when they are not saved and much more! It is time for you to receive healing and for God to use you to administer healing to others!

Enjoy the Devotional!

Dr. Kevin L. Zadai
Founder and President of Warrior Notes and Warrior Notes School of Ministry

DR. KEVIN L. ZADAI

DAY 1

Restored to Your Youth

Then He is gracious to him, and says, 'Deliver him from going down to the Pit; I have found a ransom'; His flesh shall be young like a child's; He shall return to the days of his youth.

—Job 33:24, 25

God has found a ransom. He found a person who could take the place of human beings and redeem them. That person was Jesus Christ. He has taken your place, and restoration is coming to your flesh. You are going to be restored to your youth. That's what God is saying in this verse.

Your flesh will be just like baby skin. Your flesh shall be fresher than that of a child, and you shall return to the days of your youth. God purchased us through Jesus Christ. He is walking amongst us and healing us. When He heals you, He is going to do an efficient job of it. It's not going to be a temporary cure or relief. He wants to heal you and restore you completely. The Word of God is true, and satan is being stopped right now in the name of Jesus.

Surrender any disbelief that has you doubting that you will receive your healing. God is the one who determines your healing, and He is restoring you right now. Write down the areas of healing you are claiming.

_____

_____

_____

_____

_____

_____

_____

_____

_____

DAY 2

Healing in His Wings

But to you who fear My name The Sun of Righteousness shall arise With healing in His wings; And you shall go out. And grow fat like stall-fed calves.

—Malachi 4:2

The Lord is saying that if you fear His name, holding it in reverence and honor, The Sun of Righteousness is going to arise, and Healing is coming from Jesus' wings. He is going to fly right in and heal you. All of this comes from you honoring God.

When He says, *"You will grow fat like stall-fed calves,"* He means that He is taking care of you. You don't have to worry about the environment or the

5

elements outside because God is protecting you. Your flesh is going to be brand new, like a baby, because God will heal you.

Present yourself to God in surrender. Accept His love for you. Honor Him for what He has done and what He will do. Write down the ways He has come through for you that you could not do in your own strength.

_____

_____

_____

_____

_____

_____

_____

_____

_____

_____

_____

DAY 3

Be Cleansed

Now a leper came to Him, imploring Him, kneeling to Him and saying to Him, "If You are willing, you can make me clean." Then Jesus, moved with compassion, stretched out His hand and touched him, and said to him, "I am willing; be cleansed. "As soon as He had spoken, immediately the leprosy left him, and he was cleansed. And He strictly warned him and sent him away at once.

—Mark 1:40-43

God has sent His Word. He sent Jesus to heal you. The fact that God has said, "You are healed," is all you need to receive healing. Jesus encountered a Centurion once, saying, "You don't even need to come to my home. If you just speak the

7

word, it shall be done" (Matthew 8:8). God is saying, "I stretched out my hand and touched him, and he was cleansed." As soon as Jesus spoke this, immediately, the leprosy left the man. God is saying to you, I've spoken, and that's good enough.

Ask Jesus the question, "If you are willing, you can make me clean." Speak aloud Jesus' response, "I am willing; be cleansed." Now receive His healing. Write down what are you experiencing after saying the words of Jesus?

_____

_____

_____

_____

_____

_____

_____

_____

_____

_____

DAY 4

Be Made Whole

When He had come down from the mountain, great multitudes followed Him. And behold, a leper came and worshiped Him, saying, "Lord, if You are willing, You can make me clean." Then Jesus put out His hand and touched him, saying, "I am willing; be cleansed." Immediately his leprosy was cleansed.

—Matthew 8:1-3

In this story, Jesus is showing us that it's God's will for you to be well. He said, "I am willing, be cleansed." When Jesus came to the Earth, He only did the will of the Father. You never see Jesus making anyone sick. You never see Him turning

9

anyone away. He healed all those who were oppressed by the devil (Acts 10:38).

If you have been asking the Lord whether He is willing to make you whole, the answer is yes! We know that God can heal, but it is His will for you to be well and made whole. He's saying, "I am not only willing and able, but I want to heal you." He is reaching out to you right now and touching you in the name of Jesus. Be ye healed.

When Jesus held out His hand and spoke, the man was immediately healed. Receive your immediate healing in Jesus' name. Write about what you encounter in the presence of the Lord.

_____

_____

_____

_____

_____

_____

_____

_____

_____

DAY 5

Health to our Flesh

My son give attention to my words; Incline your ear to my sayings. Do not let them depart from your eyes; Keep them in the midst of your heart; For they are life to those who find them, And health to all their flesh.
—Proverbs 4:20-22

Solomon wrote this verse. God had given him wisdom, but it was for our benefit that we would take in the words that he spoke. Incline your ears to hear what the Holy Spirit is saying. The wisdom that is in our hearts from the Holy Spirit is health to our flesh. We need to listen to Him.

Everything that God says through Jesus and the Holy Spirit is bringing health to you. Whenever you get a

11

good word from God, it brings encouragement. You get excited when He speaks, and it brings forth healing. It's because His Word is tangible. Paul talks about how the power that rose Jesus from the dead dwells in you, and it will quicken your mortal flesh. That power transfers in physical form to you and gives you life (Romans 8:11). The power of Jesus is electrifying and making your flesh alive right now.

Incline your ears to hear what the Father is saying. See it with your eyes, and keep what He reveals to you close to your heart. Write down what He says and shows you.

_____

_____

_____

_____

_____

_____

_____

_____

_____

_____

DAY 6

Speak to your Mountain

There is one who speaks like the piercings of a sword, But the tongue of the wise promotes health.

—Proverbs 12:18

God is telling us how important it is to watch our tongue. When we speak, we have to make sure that what we say is what we want to see take place. Here in Proverbs, it says, "Your tongue promotes health." You could be speaking of where you're going. You could be declaring that you are healed. Say it with your mouth, "I am healed."

Don't speak about your condition or about what's happening in the environment around you. Say where you are going, and declare the Word of God.

In Mark 11:23 and 24, Jesus talks about speaking to your mountain; to believe what you are saying, in your heart, and believe you've received it, and you shall have it. We can ask anything in prayer, and we will receive it, but the key is to not doubt.

As an activation, speak where it is you are going. Pay attention to what you say with your mouth throughout the day. Say those things that promote healing and abundance. Write down your declarations.

_____

_____

_____

_____

_____

_____

_____

_____

_____

_____

DAY 7

Yield to Joy

A merry heart does good, like medicine, But a broken spirit dries the bones.

—Proverbs 17:22

Did you know that there is a physical-chemical response that takes place in your body when you yield to joy and laughter? When you make yourself happy, it's your will deciding that you're going to be pleased. Being merry and happy is medicine, and you want to take your medication today. Here in Proverbs, it talks about the heart of man.

Even if you can't see all that God is doing, it doesn't mean it's not happening. He wants you to build

15

yourself up in the most holy of faith and speak out of that faith. Find something to laugh about and be joyful. The Holy Spirit wants to bring joy to you always. Yield to that joy, "for the joy of the Lord, is your strength" (Nehemiah 8:10).

In your time of prayer, remember the things that bring you joy and peace. What do you see, and how will you purpose to make these a vital part of your daily life?

_____

_____

_____

_____

_____

_____

_____

_____

DAY 8

Shalom Peace

The Lord will give strength to His people;
The Lord will bless His people with peace
—Psalm 29:11

G od wants to give you strength and bless you with His peace today. The peace from Heaven is called *Shalom*. It's the kind of peace that settles you so that you don't worry anymore. God comes and meets your needs from the Heavenly realm. He calls the shots like an umpire in a game. He says, "Stop; this is the way it's going to be now." When God's *Shalom* peace comes, its purpose is to correct things.

No matter what is going on in your body or your life today, God is coming as an umpire and saying, "this is not right," and He's throwing it out. He's throwing out sickness right now. He's giving you peace and bringing you into correction.

If there's anything in your life that needs to be recompensed, He will provide. If your heart needs to be restored, He will bring you the healing and peace you need. He is strengthening and encouraging you from within, and He's driving the devil out of your life. Be encouraged and give God the glory.

Are there any areas in your life that need to be lit up with the peace of God? Pray for His peace to come to every part of your body. Declare for His peace to reign in the environment in which you live. Write about your encounter.

_____

_____

_____

_____

_____

_____

_____

_____

DAY 9

A Faithful God

Lord my God, I called to you for help, And you healed me.

—Psalm 30:2 NIV

Here, the Psalmist explains how faithful God is. When he cried out for help and asked God to heal him, the Lord answered and healed him. How long have you been waiting for God to heal you? The power of God is so strong that it's reaching out to you. The Lord wants to heal you.

He said Jesus came and healed all that were oppressed by the devil. He went around healing everyone. When He died, He redeemed mankind, but He also brought healing for you. Thank God for your healing. What the doctors couldn't do and what you

19

couldn't do yourself, God wants to do for you! Miracles are coming from the throne of God. Rivers of life are flowing out right now into your heart, body, and mind. Receive His healing right now.

In your prayer time, call out for help from the Lord for any area of your body, mind, or heart that needs the healing touch of God. If you have already encountered healing, worship Him, and thank Him for what He has done.

_____

_____

_____

_____

_____

_____

_____

_____

_____

_____

_____

DAY 10

God is Preserving You

The Lord will preserve him and keep him alive, And he will be blessed on the Earth; You will not deliver him to the will of his enemies.

—Psalm 41:2

God's will for you is to live and not die. He is willing to preserve you and keep you alive. No matter what the devil has planned for you, it doesn't matter because God gives you the strength to live a long and prosperous life. The power that rose Jesus from the dead caused His body to come back to life. When Jesus went to funerals, He ruined them, like in the story of Lazarus. He said, "oh, he's not dead; he's just sleeping" (John 11:11) Jesus raised Lazarus from the dead, and his body came alive.

21

God is preserving your life. You can't always see what He's doing, but He works on your behalf. Trust that He's preserving you and giving you strength.

Pray and soak in God's presence. Ask the Lord to renew your mind to the truth of His Word. Reject all thoughts or ideas that are contrary to the Word of God. Write down any scriptures that God brings up in your spirit.

_____

_____

_____

_____

_____

_____

_____

_____

_____

_____

_____

DAY 11

The Help of our Countenance

Why are you cast down, O my soul? And why are you disquieted within me? Hope in God; For I shall yet praise Him, The help of my countenance and my God.

—Psalm 42:11

Here, David is talking to himself, saying, "What is wrong with me inside?" He is contemplating why he is feeling a certain way. We can relate to David, and we may have said to ourselves, "I just don't understand myself." Often it is because we don't understand how God made us.

He made us spiritual beings, which means we have an inner spiritual part that lives forever. It's the part of us that becomes born again when we accept Jesus.

However, we also have a soul, which is our mind, will, and emotions. At times, your soul does not line up with your spirit and God's Spirit. David was saying, "listen, soul, you need to shape up. Why are you so disquieted and cast down?"

You can speak to your soul from your heart and your spirit and say, "You need to get happy and start looking at all the good things that God has done for you." David said, "God, you are the help of my countenance." Your countenance is your smile. God wants you to smile. He's saying, be happy, and receive the joy of the Lord.

Reflect on the wonderful things God has done in your life. Write them down.

_____

_____

_____

_____

_____

_____

_____

DAY 12

God is Protecting You

When you sit enthroned under the shadow of Shaddai, you are hidden in the strength of God Most High. He's the hope that holds me and the Stronghold to shelter me, the only God for me, and my great confidence. He will rescue you from every hidden trap of the enemy, and he will protect you from false accusation and any deadly curse. His massive arms are wrapped around you, protecting you. You can run under his covering of majesty and hide. His arms of faithfulness are a shield keeping you from harm.

—Psalm 91:1-4 TPT

At times, you may feel like there's a curse working against you, but God is protecting you and keeping you from any curse. He is protecting you from these false curses that come against you. Every curse is broken, and God has sent His Word to heal you. Receive your healing and be encouraged. He is with you in a mighty way.

Whatever concerns you have, His protection assures you. He has the solution. Ask for His wisdom and write down what He shows you.

_____

_____

_____

_____

_____

_____

_____

_____

_____

_____

_____

DAY 13

The Benefits of Relationship with God

Bless the Lord, O my soul, And forget not all His benefits: Who forgives all your iniquities, Who heals all your diseases, Who redeems your life from destruction, Who crowns you with lovingkindness, and tender mercies.
—Psalm 103:2-4

David is saying that God has given us many benefits. We can count on His benefits and know that He forgives and heals us. He redeems us and crowns us with lovingkindness. This is the heart of the Father. He created us so that we could stand face to face and be in fellowship and communion with Him.

27

He is redeeming us and bringing us back from the fall through Jesus Christ. You are becoming like Him more and more every day. He wants you to receive His healing today.

Meditate on today's verse. Read it aloud and let it resonate within you until you see a shift in you. Write about the peace you encounter.

_____

_____

_____

_____

_____

_____

_____

_____

_____

_____

_____

DAY 14

You are Healed

He sent His Word and healed them, And delivered them from their destructions.
—Psalm 107:20

God is sending you a word, and He's saying, "I want to announce to you that you are healed." You don't have to wait any longer for your healing. God has given you His Word. He sent Jesus, who is the Word. The destructions that were planned for you are canceled.

Every curse against you is broken in Jesus' name. All sickness has to leave you, and the power of the enemy is broken and driven out. You are healed. Receive your healing right now in the name of Jesus.

When you go into prayer today, meditate on these words, "I am healed." Believe what the Psalmist David is saying. You are healed and delivered by the Word of God. Write about the healing you receive today.

_____

_____

_____

_____

_____

_____

_____

_____

_____

_____

_____

_____

_____

_____

DAY 15

I Will Heal You

"Return and tell Hezekiah the leader of My people, 'Thus says the Lord, the God of David, your father: "I have heard your prayer, I have seen your tears; surely I will heal you. On the third day you shall go up to the house of the Lord.

—2 Kings 20:5

God is saying, I have heard your prayers, I've listened to your cry, and I'm going to answer you and heal you. Whenever Jesus shows up, He always wants to heal, and He always has something good to say.

He's reaching His hand out to you right now and asking you, "Will you receive your healing?" Believe in your heart and not with your head. Say, "Thank you, Lord, I receive my healing today." He's heard your prayers, and He's seen your tears. Realize that God is answering you. Receive your healing from Him.

In prayer, surrender your worries to God. He hears you. Write down what you have given to the Father today.

_____

_____

_____

_____

_____

_____

_____

_____

_____

_____

_____

_____

DAY 16

Jesus Heals All

How God anointed Jesus of Nazareth with the Holy Spirit and with power, who went about doing good and healing all who were oppressed by the devil for God was with Him.
—Acts 10:38

God's will for you is to be well. He used Jesus on the earth to heal the sick and set people free. Jesus said, "I don't do anything unless I see my Father doing it. I don't say anything unless my Father is saying it" (John 5:19). God is saying to you today that through Jesus, "I drove out sickness and healed everyone, and I want to heal you."

Jesus broke the power of sickness at the cross, and He is seated at the right hand of God. He's saying,

33

"You don't have to be sick anymore." There are miracles of healing flowing from the throne to you. All sickness has to go in Jesus' name, and the devil is being driven out of your life. The Lord is healing you right now. Receive it!

Worship Jesus for coming to the earth, dying on the cross, and setting you free. Worship Him for healing you and bringing you peace. Thank the Lord for sending Jesus and express your gratitude below.

_____

_____

_____

_____

_____

_____

_____

_____

_____

_____

DAY 17

God Extends your Life

That your days and the days of your children may be multiplied in the land of which the Lord swore to your fathers to give them, like the days of the heavens above the earth.
—Deuteronomy 11:21

God wants to prolong your life. He wants to extend it out, but not just for you, for your children as well. He's multiplying your days, and His purpose is to bless you. You don't have to encounter anything that will cut your life short. You are going to live a long and prosperous life.

The body of Christ needs you. There is so much the Lord wants to do through you on the Earth. He is making you well and extending His hand to heal you.

When you go into prayer today, purpose to talk with the Lord about the plans He has for you. What has He asked you to do while you are on the earth? Write down what He shares with you.

_____

_____

_____

_____

_____

_____

_____

_____

_____

_____

_____

DAY 18

God Gives You Strength

Your sandals shall be iron and bronze; As your days, so shall our strength be.
—Deuteronomy 33:25

As your days go in length, so shall your strength be. God is guaranteeing that as long as you're alive on the earth, you will encounter strength. He's not going to back off, and He's not going to stop helping you. He will always be there for you. The Holy Spirit is known as the Standby (John 14:26 AMP). He's like auxiliary power.

When electricity fluctuates in intensity, a generator kicks in and supports what is lacking. That's what the Holy Spirit does. In our weakness, He comes in and brings us up to the level we should be. God is going to be the strength you need for your entire life. He's going to help you. He's quickening your body. It's as if electricity is going through you as you're being healed in the name of Jesus.

In what areas of your life do you need to be strengthened by the Holy Spirit? Ask Him to minister to you and provide you with power. Write about what He shows you.

_____

_____

_____

_____

_____

_____

_____

_____

_____

_____

DAY 19

The Lord Takes Away Sickness

And the Lord will take away from you all sickness and will afflict you with none of the terrible diseases of Egypt which you have known but will lay them on all those who hate you.

—Deuteronomy 7:15

The Lord is taking sickness away from you. He's not only taking it, but He's giving it to those who hate you. When someone comes against you, they're coming against God. You are a child of God, and He is very protective over you.

Egypt represents a type or nature of the world. You're not going to be afflicted like the world because you are not of it. Let the world deal with their problems themselves, but you receive your healing.

We know that it's through Jesus Christ that we receive healing. All the suffering He went through on the cross was to take sickness upon Himself so that we don't have to bear it anymore. Believe what the scripture says, for the Lord is taking sickness away from you.

Present your concerns to the Lord. Thank Him for His protection and healing power. How has He provided His peace to you in the middle of your circumstances?

_____

_____

_____

_____

_____

_____

_____

_____

_____

DAY 20

God Turns Curses into Blessings

Nevertheless, the Lord your God would not listen to Balaam, but the Lord your God turned the curse into a blessing for you, because the Lord your God loves you.
—Deuteronomy 23:5

God turned these Old Testament curses into blessings, and He will do the same for you. He's the same yesterday, today, and forever. He can take whatever the enemy has presented you with and turn it into a blessing.

You can say, "I don't accept it; it's a curse. God wants to bless me, and He will turn this curse into a blessing because He loves me." God is inside of you, and He is correcting what isn't right. He is giving you the authority to drive out the devil and say, "devil, you are not going to curse me anymore. The Lord blesses me."

Speak to the circumstances of your life with the authority God has given you. You can use the examples here in today's devotional as a guide. Write what you encountered after speaking with authority.

_____

_____

_____

_____

_____

_____

_____

_____

_____

_____

DAY 21

Christ Redeemed Us from the Curse

Christ has redeemed us from the curse of the law, having become a curse for us (for it is written, "Cursed is everyone who hangs on a tree"), that the blessing of Abraham might come upon the Gentiles in Christ Jesus, that we might receive the promise of the Spirit through faith.

—Galatians 3:13

Jesus has redeemed us from sickness. Every plague that has to do with the curse, God has redeemed from us through Jesus Christ. When Jesus was on the earth, He only healed people. He did not make people sick.

He's seated at the right hand of God speaking for you. He took every sickness upon Himself, and He's turning to the Father and saying, "No, I healed them. I took that upon myself, so they don't have to be sick."

Claim your healing as you are in prayer. Say to the Lord, "You've redeemed me from the curse. You broke poverty and sickness. I am well, and I receive it in the name of Jesus." How has declaring these truths helped you?

_____

_____

_____

_____

_____

_____

_____

_____

_____

_____

_____

DAY 22

The Plague Shall not be upon You

Now the blood shall be a sign for you on the houses where you are. And when I see the blood, I will pass over you; and the plague shall not be on you to destroy you when I strike the land of Egypt.

—Exodus 12:13

This verse talks about the night the angel of death came to those living in Egypt. The plague intended to destroy the firstborn children. If the blood was on the doorpost, it meant that the angel of death had to pass over them.

Now we have the blood of Jesus, and the blood of Jesus has marked the doorpost of our heart so that death has to pass over us. The effects of sin are a plague. All curses and the effects caused by sin have been completely taken care of through the blood of Jesus, but the effects of sin still have to be taken away from a believer. The plague doesn't have to touch your dwelling place because Jesus put the blood from His own body on your doorpost so that the plague has to pass over. We will still die, but we can live a lot longer because God wants us to be on the Earth and in good health.

Accept the protection of the Lord. Thank Him for what Jesus has done by giving you His blood to cover you. If there is any sin in your life, repent and turn from it. Give it over to God. Receive His mercy and grace. Let your heart be glad for He cares for you.

_____

_____

_____

_____

_____

_____

_____

DAY 23

The Lord Heals You

"If you diligently heed the voice of the Lord your God and do what is right in His sight, give ear to His commandments and keep all His statutes, I will put none of the diseases on you which I have brought on the Egyptians. For I am the Lord who heals you."

—Exodus 15:26

God is the one who heals you. He is the one who has sent His Word so that you have restoration. He promises today that you do not have to suffer. The Lord is sending His Word to you today, and He's saying, "Release your cares to me. I know that you're going through a lot, and I have taken it upon myself. Do not fear."

Jesus took the stripes upon His back and suffered and died so that He could heal you. He bore so much for you to be free. Walk in this freedom today and receive your healing.

When you go into prayer today, purpose to clear any worry from your mind. If there is any doubt, release it to God and ask Him to fill you with His truth and wisdom. Write what He shares with you.

_____

_____

_____

_____

_____

_____

_____

_____

_____

_____

DAY 24

The Lord takes Sickness Away

So, you shall serve the Lord your God, and He will bless your bread and your water. And I will take sickness away from the midst of you.

—Exodus 23:25

He's going to bless you because He is your God. It says here, "*He will bless your bread and your water*," which is your sustenance, your food, and your nourishment. He will take sickness away from the midst of you.

In the New Testament, we, as Christians, believe in the covenant of healing through Jesus Christ. God has taken away sickness from you through Jesus Christ. The blood of Jesus and the suffering He went

49

through on the cross removes sickness from your body. Believe what His Word says and receive your healing right now in the name of Jesus.

Write down the ways God has blessed you so far? Know that He will continue to bless you.

_____

_____

_____

_____

_____

_____

_____

_____

_____

_____

_____

_____

DAY 25

You Shall Live 120 Years

And the Lord said, "My Spirit shall not strive with man forever, for he is indeed flesh; yet his days shall be one hundred and twenty years."

—Genesis 6:3

God spoke and put a limitation on how long we can live. During the time of the flood, He was grieved, and He commanded Noah to build the Ark. God said, "It's going to be 120 years, and that's as long as a man will live." If you can reach 100 years old today, you are considered amazing and of old age. Before the flood, people lived to be 800 and 900 years old. God made man, and He made them eternal

51

beings. When Adam and Eve fell and were cast out of the garden, they lived to be 930 years old.

God promises that we can live a long life. He has ordained you to come to full fruition. If you have a disease or life-threatening illness that is trying to take your life in a shorter period of time than what God has ordained, it's the enemy trying to take you out early. That curse is broken in Jesus' name. God assured us 120 years by His Word.

> *Now, as for you, you shall go to your fathers in peace; you shall be buried at a good old age.*
>
> —Genesis 15:15

Meditate on what God's Word says, that you will live 120 years. See yourself living a healthy life, enjoying your family and friends.

_____

_____

_____

_____

_____

DAY 26

He Took our Place

*Surely He has borne our griefs. And carried
our sorrows; Yet we esteemed Him stricken,
Smitten by God, and afflicted.*

—Isaiah 53:4

Everything Jesus did for us when He went to the cross, and the affliction He took was so that we could be healed. When Jesus redeemed us, it wasn't only so we could go to Heaven; it was because we needed healing down here. Jesus Himself carried our griefs and our sicknesses. He was afflicted and smitten by God so that we wouldn't have to be. He took our place and was wounded and bruised so that we would be healed. God didn't create this world with disease; He created us to be well. He never wanted you to be sick. He wants you to walk in good health.

Meditate on today's scripture and receive what Jesus did on the cross for you 2000 years ago. Encounter God's grace for you in prayer. Write down your experience.

_____

_____

_____

_____

_____

_____

_____

_____

_____

_____

_____

_____

DAY 27

I Will Recover You

The lame will leap like a deer, and those who cannot speak will sing for joy! Springs will gush forth in the wilderness, and streams will water the wasteland.

—Isaiah 35:6 NLT

This verse is a prophecy that was given to Isaiah to speak forth. In these last days, we're going to see people who have been bound in wheelchairs, walkers, and canes, be freed and healed. God will manifest His goodness and kindness onto people and heal them. The Lord is speaking through the prophet Isaiah here, but He's speaking to you right now, so receive these words.

Let the power of the Lord Jesus Christ restore whatever is broken in your body. He's recovering you and making you live. The influence of satan over your life is broken, and evil spirits are driven out in Jesus' name. The Spirit of God is healing you right now. Begin to thank Him for your healing.

> *O Lord, by these things men live; And in all these things is the life of my spirit; So You will restore me and make me live.*
> —Isaiah 38:16

Visualize, speak, and meditate on today's verse. Picture yourself leaping and singing with rivers of living water flowing out of you. See yourself healed and thank the Lord. Write about what you see.

_____

_____

_____

_____

_____

_____

_____

DAY 28

He Increases our Strength

But those who wait on the Lord Shall renew their strength; They shall mount up with wings like eagles, They shall run and not be weary, They shall walk and not faint.
—Isaiah 40:3

God is the healer, and He is increasing your strength. He is giving you power, and you're not going to faint. God is restoring, renewing, and quickening your mortal body. He is renewing your strength just like the Eagles, and He's causing you to go above all your troubles. He is strengthening you and helping you. That is His promise.

Jesus healed everyone who came to Him, and He will do it for you. He is determined to heal and deliver

57

you of all your troubles today. Go to Him now and receive your healing by His power.

He giveth power to the faint; and to them that have no might he increaseth strength.
—Isaiah 40:29 KJV

In prayer today, believe that you will receive what you're asking God for, and you shall have it (Mark 11:24). Write down the prayer God is answering today.

_____

_____

_____

_____

_____

_____

_____

_____

_____

DAY 29

I will Carry and Deliver You

Even to your old age, I am He, And even to gray hairs I will carry you! I have made, and I will bear; Even I will carry and will deliver you.

—Isaiah 46:4

G od is promising that no matter what age you are, He's going to help you. As you get older and have gray hair, He's going to carry you, and He will deliver you. There are times where you can't do things yourself, and you need to rely on the Lord. Allow yourself to get to the place where you let the Lord help you. Let Him speak to you. Let Him carry you through your troubles. You don't have to do this alone. No matter how old you are, God promises to help you and be with you until the very end. Rely on

His breath to breathe on you, whatever it is that you need.

He's renewing your strength, and all pain is leaving your body. If you have pain in your neck, shoulders, or your lower back, you will experience relief now in the name of Jesus. He is healing your ankles and legs and any arthritis right now. Begin to thank Him for healing you.

How has The Lord caused you to view healing in a new way?

_____

_____

_____

_____

_____

_____

_____

_____

DAY 30

By His Stripes, You are Healed

But He was wounded for our transgressions, He was bruised for our iniquities; The chastisement for our peace was upon Him, And by His stripes we are healed.

—Isaiah 53:5

Did you know that the stripes of Jesus healed you? You were healed Two-Thousand years ago. Did you know that even before that, Jesus determined that He was coming back? He was slain from the foundation of the world. When Jesus was in eternity with God before this earth was made, He decided on the plan of salvation. In that plan of salvation, there was healing. You were healed before the Earth was even formed. Jesus died on the cross and took beatings upon Himself, and the Word says

61

that the stripes from the cat of nine tails that Jesus took on His back were enough to heal you. By His stripes, you were healed. The Lord promises us in Isaiah 57:19, "I will heal you." He stands by His promises. Receive your healing in the name of Jesus.

Is there anything holding you back from believing the words of Jesus? Present it to the Father and determine in your heart to receive what He has said and done. He won't go back on His word.

_____

_____

_____

_____

_____

_____

_____

_____

_____

_____

_____

DAY 31

Your Healing will Spring Forth Speedily

Then your light shall break forth like the morning, Your healing shall spring forth speedily, And your righteousness shall go before you; The glory of the LORD shall be your rear guard.

—Isaiah 58:8

What's happening to you right now is like the breaking of the dawn when the sun starts to come up, and darkness is dispelled. Health is being restored to you. Your health is in the hands of God, and He wants to give you healing. The power of the Holy Spirit is resting on you, and everything you need for life and godliness has been given to you through God's promises. One of those promises is that your light is breaking forth as the morning, and

He is providing you with healing. It is coming speedily towards you right now in the name of Jesus. He is restoring you!

Worship Him and thank Him for healing you in advance. As you encounter His presence, what are you experiencing in your body, mind, or spirit right now?

_____

_____

_____

_____

_____

_____

_____

_____

_____

_____

DAY 32

God is Restoring Your Health

For I will restore health to you And heal you of your wounds,' says the Lord, 'Because they called you an outcast saying: "This is Zion; No one seeks her."

—Jeremiah 30:17

The Lord said, through the prophet Jeremiah, that He will restore health to you and heal your wounds. This is a promise from God. Every time you read a scripture, it is the very Word of God for your life; it is timeless. All you have to do is turn your face toward Jesus, reach out, and let Him touch you. By His power, He is delivering you from the hand of the enemy and destroying the works of the devil. Whatever it is that you need healing for, receive it from the Lord.

65

Declare the Word of the Lord over yourself. Declare that He is restoring health to you and healing you of your wounds. Express in words what you encounter in prayer.

_____

_____

_____

_____

_____

_____

_____

_____

_____

_____

_____

DAY 33

Health and a Cure

*Behold, I will bring it health and cure, and I
will cure them, and will reveal unto them the
abundance of peace and truth.*
　　　　　　　　　　—Jeremiah 33:6 KJV

The Lord has made a promise to us through the
prophet Jeremiah that He's coming to us. When
He comes, He's bringing with Him healing and a
cure. He's going to care for us and establish His
righteous decree in our lives. God will reveal the
abundance of His peace and truth. He will not
withhold His perfect will from you. Lift your hands
and receive all that God has spoken through
Jeremiah.

What does it look like to live from God's peace and truth every day? How will you commit to it, and what changes will you make to stay in God's presence?

_____

_____

_____

_____

_____

_____

_____

_____

_____

_____

_____

_____

_____

_____

DAY 34

He Binds and Strengthens

"I will seek that which was lost, and bring again that which was driven away, and will bind up that which was broken, and will strengthen that which was sick: but I will destroy the fat and the strong; I will feed them with judgment."

—Ezekiel 34:16 KJV

The Lord is saying that He will bind up anything in your life that is broken. Anything in your body that is causing you pain, the Lord is coming to fix it. He's addressing it. He wants to help you and encourage you today. Receive the breath of God. Receive the Word of the Lord through Ezekiel that you are restored right now in your body.

69

Whatever it is that you're going through, look to the Lord, for He is your healer. He's the one that has the solution for you. Trust in Him. Receive the healing anointing of Jesus right now.

Express to the Lord your gratitude for healing you. Thank Him for sending Jesus, who suffered for your sins and sickness. Thank Him for taking the beatings upon His back for you. Write about your thankfulness.

_____

_____

_____

_____

_____

_____

_____

_____

_____

_____

DAY 35

The Breath of God

Thus says the Lord GOD to these bones: Behold, I will cause breath to enter you, and you shall live...

And I will put my Spirit within you, and you shall live, and I will place you in your own land. Then you shall know that I am the LORD; I have spoken, and I will do it, declares the LORD."

—Ezekiel 37:5,14 ESV

The Holy Spirit is the breath of God. He is the *Ruach Ha Kodesh*— The Spirit of Holiness. He is the breath of the Almighty God. There is resurrection power in His spirit, and you will live because life is in His breath. Healing is in His breath.

71

Jesus suffered and died so that you can receive healing in your body. Don't let anyone rob you of what God has done for you. He died so that you would live.

What we have to do is meditate on the breath of God every day and receive it. His breath causes clarity in your mind, and it brings strength and healing to your body.

Picture Jesus and the Father breathing life and strength into you. Tell the Father that you receive the power and breath of the Holy Spirit in the name of Jesus. Enter into life with Him.

_____

_____

_____

_____

_____

_____

_____

_____

_____

DAY 36

The River of Life

And it shall be that every living thing that moves, wherever the rivers go, will live. There will be a very great multitude of fish, because these waters go there; for they will be healed, and everything will live wherever the river goes.

—Ezekiel 47:9

The River of Life is flowing from the throne of God. There is eternal life in that water. Wherever that river goes, there is life and healing. The River of Life is what gives you everlasting life, and you're going to live forever in God's kingdom. In John 7:38, Jesus said that there are rivers of living water coming out of your belly. The River of Life inside of you is the Spirit of God. The Spirit of God

73

that is in you is healing you right now. In other words, you're being healed through the River of Life, and it's flowing from you. Your doctors will not have an explanation for the miraculous power of God that is working in your life. You're going to have a good report; receive your healing right now.

Envision the River of Life flowing from the throne room of God and that the same river is inside of you. Wherever that river goes, there is healing and life. Let that reality settle in you. Write about what you encounter with the Holy Spirit.

_____

_____

_____

_____

_____

_____

_____

_____

_____

_____

DAY 37

Seek the Lord

For thus saith the LORD unto the house of Israel, Seek ye me, and ye shall live.

—Amos 5:4 KJV

These are promises that God gives us, that those who diligently seek God will be rewarded. He is a rewarder of those who diligently seek Him (Hebrews 11:6). When we seek God, we will encounter eternal life. God is there to intervene and help you no matter what is going on in your body or mind, but you must do your part by seeking Him.

Diligently seek God through the scriptures. Pray and ask for His help. Thank Him for your healing. He is there to intervene, and He wants to restore your flesh. God wants you to be strong so that you can do His mighty work.

In your time of prayer and seeking, cry out to Him and say, "Lord, I receive you. I need you, and I want to know your healing power. Let Him minister to you. Write about what He shows you.

_____

_____

_____

_____

_____

_____

_____

_____

_____

DAY 38

There is Healing in His Wings

But for you who fear my name, the Sun of Righteousness will rise with healing in his wings. And you will go free, leaping with joy like calves let out to pasture.

—Malachi 4:2 NLT

Jesus fulfilled this promise. He came and walked the earth, healing all that were oppressed of the devil (Acts 10:38). God, through Jesus Christ, is healing people today. Did you know there is healing in God's wings, and beams of light come from Him? When He smiles at you, the light from His face has healing power in it. His favor is shining upon you.

Jesus never turned anyone away that came to Him. When people said to Him, "If you're willing, you can make me well?" He said, "I am willing" (Matthew 8:2). The Bible says that all things are possible to Him that believes (Mark 9:23). Do you believe that God can heal you? God isn't doubtful about your healing. He knows you need it. Receive His supernatural healing power today in Jesus' name.

When you pray today, claim your healing. God has spoken that He is willing to heal you. Come into agreement with what He is saying and believe. See yourself leaping with joy with your healing, as they did in Malachi 4:2.

_____

_____

_____

_____

_____

_____

_____

_____

_____

_____

DAY 39

Jesus has Compassion for You

And when Jesus went out He saw a great multitude; and He was moved with compassion for them, and healed their sick.
—Matthew 14:14

Jesus was moved with compassion for people. He desired to heal anyone who came in contact with Him. He feels that way for you. No matter what situation you find yourself in, you can rely on Jesus. He walked the earth and went around doing good and healing everyone that was oppressed by the devil. He is affected by how you've been coping with your infirmities. He knows what you're going through, and He wants to heal you.

How does it make you feel that Jesus has compassion for you? In prayer today, be open to receiving His love. Write about His kindness towards you.

_____

_____

_____

_____

_____

_____

_____

_____

_____

_____

_____

_____

_____

_____

_____

DAY 40

Jesus Healed Every Disease

And Jesus went about all Galilee, teaching in their synagogues, and preaching the gospel of the kingdom, and healing all manner of sickness and all manner of disease among the people.

—Matthew 4:23 KJV

The Lord went all around, doing good, healing everyone, and every kind of disease. He is still the healer today, and He has compassion for you. He has destroyed the works of the devil, which means that any kind of sickness or disease that is attacking you right now, God wants to heal. The Lord is with you, and He's burning out every disease and virus. with His fire. He is driving out sickness right now in the name of Jesus!

81

Reflect on the fact that Jesus healed all manner of sickness and disease. You are not exempt from the healing He wants to complete in you. Write what Jesus shows you or speaks to you about this today.

_____

_____

_____

_____

_____

_____

_____

_____

_____

_____

_____

_____

_____

DAY 41

Be it Unto You

*Then He touched their eyes, saying,
"According to your faith be it unto you."*
—Matthew 9:29 KJV

Jesus went around doing good. When He would ask people what they wanted, they would tell Him, and He would say, "Be it according to your faith. Where is your level of trust, and how much can you believe God for right now? Jesus is not limiting you. There is nothing in Heaven that is limiting you. You are only limited by how you think and how you believe.

The Lord is saying, "Be it unto you as your faith has allowed." What are you allowing God to do in your life? Are you allowing Him to reach out and touch you and heal you? That is what He wants to do. He is asking you, "where is your faith?" God is reaching out to you. He is building up your faith by giving you His Word and His Spirit. When those two things come together within our human spirit, it produces faith. Faith comes by hearing and hearing the word of the Lord (2 Corinthians 5:17). God has sent His word to heal you. Receive it by faith.

Get rid of any doubt that would stop you from believing God's Word. Write down any scriptures the Lord directs you to.

_____

_____

_____

_____

_____

_____

_____

_____

_____

_____

DAY 42

Power and Authority

And when He had called His twelve disciples to Him, He gave them power over unclean spirits, to cast them out, and to heal all kinds of sickness and all kinds of disease.

—Matthew 10:1

Jesus gave the disciples the authority to drive out evil spirits. He said I give you power and authority over unclean spirits to cast them out and heal them. Not only did Jesus heal and drive out devils, but He gave us the power to do it as well. We know that the twelve disciples did this and that the 70 who were sent out accomplished this as well. Before Jesus left, He told us to go out and do the same. He said that we were going to do the work that He did. The Lord has anointed you heal the sick, drive out devils, raise the dead, and preach the good news. If you have something in your own body that is bothering you, such as any physical pain or disease, you can lay your hands on yourself and command your body to be well. Jesus gave this power to you to use in His name.

Go into the marketplace today and pray for the sick. Believe that when you say the name of Jesus, devils are going to leave. You will see healing manifest.

_____

_____

_____

_____

_____

_____

_____

_____

_____

_____

_____

DAY 43

Perfectly Whole

And besought him that they might only touch the hem of his garment: and as many as touched were made perfectly whole.
—Matthew 14:36 KJV

Everyone that Jesus touched, He made perfectly whole. He never failed to see anyone that came to Him. He wants to make you perfectly whole. The power of the Holy Spirit is in the words written in Matthew 14:36. The name of Jesus is mighty. Speak the name of Jesus and command sickness to go. Tell every foul lying devil to leave your body in Jesus' name. Receive your healing and deliverance today.

Your wholeness rests on a touch from Jesus. Begin to worship Him and receive His presence and power. Let Him minister to the deepest parts of you. Write down your encounter with Jesus.

_____

_____

_____

_____

_____

_____

_____

_____

_____

_____

_____

_____

DAY 44

Healing is the Children's Bread

But He answered and said, "It is not good to take the children's bread and throw it to the little dogs."

Matthew 15:26

J esus said that Healing is the children's bread. He was talking about the covenant. In the Old Testament, God took sickness away from the midst of all the children of Israel. Through a covenant with them, He promised that He would take them out of Egypt and bring them into the land of plenty, into the Promised Land.

Jesus' name in Hebrew is Joshua. In the Old Testament, Joshua took the people out of Egypt and into the Promised Land, where they received their

89

inheritance. Through the cross, Jesus has taken us out of the world, out of Egypt, and brought us into the Promised Land. Healing is part of the provision we have received. Healing is the children's bread. As a child of God, we have every right to eat the healing bread, the manna that came down from Heaven. Did you know that you are in The Promised Land? You are there because God's covenant is working.

Picture yourself eating the bread of healing! Because you dwell in the Promised Land, you may eat of the bread. God is taking sickness away and confirming His covenant with you. Receive your healing!

_____

_____

_____

_____

_____

_____

_____

_____

DAY 45

Jesus does the Work of the Father

And they were astonished beyond measure saying, "He has done all things well. He makes both the deaf to hear, and the mute to speak.

—Mark 7:37

Jesus would go to various towns and teach the people. He would tell them that the Father had sent Him and that He was doing the work of His Father. He would complete these works by driving out devils and laying hands on the sick. People would recover right there in front of all that were watching.

They would dance around and rejoice at the healings they received or witnessed. Those that couldn't speak; their tongues were loosed, and the deaf would hear. Jesus went around doing good, and miracles broke out. He is still healing in the same way today. You might be encountering pain right now, or maybe you've endured sickness for a long time; Jesus is willing to heal you. He hasn't changed, and He is demonstrating the love of God. Receive it right now.

Write about a time that you experienced a miracle from God? Express how happy it made you feel.

_____

_____

_____

_____

_____

_____

_____

_____

_____

_____

_____

_____

DAY 46

The Great Commission

They will take up serpents; and if they drink anything deadly, it will by no means hurt them; they will lay hands on the sick, and they will recover."

—Mark 16:18

Jesus told all of us, not only the disciples that we are to go forth with the great commission and preach the Word of God. We are to preach the good news of the gospel, lay hands on the sick, and they will recover, and command devils to leave. He's saying that people can be commanded to come back from the dead. We are to do all of these things.

93

We are going to do these works because we believe. We are the believing ones. Jesus promised us that He is working with us, confirming the Word of God through miracles, signs, and wonders.

Today, as you go out, pray for someone to receive healing. Even those who are unsaved can receive healing from God. Tell them about Jesus and what He has done for them. Write about your day.

_____

_____

_____

_____

_____

_____

_____

_____

_____

_____

_____

DAY 47

The Healing Power of God

"The Spirit of the LORD is upon Me, Because He has anointed Me To preach the gospel to the poor; He has sent Me to heal the brokenhearted, To proclaim liberty to the captives And recovery of sight to the blind, To set at liberty those who are oppressed;

—Luke 4:18

The healing power of God heals the brokenhearted and delivers the captives. If you are held captive by the devil in any way, God's healing anointing will cause you to be delivered and healed. He recovers sight to the blind, and He sets at liberty those who are bruised. Jesus came to seek and save, to restore and give deliverance to those who are lost. God is not holding back His healing from you.

95

He has healing in His wings, in the beams that come from His face, and in His smile. He is shining upon you, and He wants you to be well. God wants to heal you physically and restore your soul—your mind, will, and emotions. Receive His healing now.

Meditate on these verses:
Isaiah 10:27 & Isaiah 61:1

What is the theme God is showing you from today's verses? How can you be a light and share God's healing power with friends, co-workers, and neighbors?

_____

_____

_____

_____

_____

_____

_____

_____

_____

_____

DAY 48

Jesus Came to Save

For the Son of man is not come to destroy men's lives, but to save them.
—Luke 9:56a KJV

Jesus explained to the people that He had come not to destroy men's lives but to save them. The Son of God came in the flesh, walked amongst us to destroy the works of the devil, not to destroy man. He even said that hell wasn't made for a man but the devil and his angels. God doesn't want anyone to perish; He wants everyone to come to eternal life. He wants to correct us in our thinking.

He wants us to know that He has come to seek and to save those who are lost. The devil's work is to kill, steal, and destroy. Jesus has come to give life and life

97

more abundantly. Right now, in the name of Jesus, receive restoration, receive healing, and receive deliverance in Jesus' name. God is intervening and causing His glorious presence to overwhelm you. Deliverance and healing have come by the power of the living God, and He will have His way in you.

Give God access to heal you and make you whole. Open your heart and allow Him in. Surrender all that keeps you bound, making room for Him. Write down how the Lord is touching you today.

_____

_____

_____

_____

_____

_____

_____

_____

_____

_____

_____

DAY 49

Power in Jesus' Name

Behold, I give you the authority to trample on serpents and scorpions, and over all the power of the enemy, and nothing shall by any means hurt you.

—Luke 10:19

Jesus is quoting part of Psalms 91 in this verse. He is telling us that we can trample on serpents and scorpions, and nothing by any means can harm us. Jesus is the fulfillment of everything in the Old Testament. The name of Jesus has given us this power. Proclaim the name of Jesus against sickness and disease.

Speak His name against any lies the devil tries to use to mess with you. Break any curses spoken over you with the name of Jesus. You have the power and authority given by Jesus to use against the enemy. According to the scriptures, you can trust in His name, and nothing shall harm you. As a Saint, you receive your glorious inheritance from the Father. Healing is a part of the inheritance that He gives. Receive it right now.

Exercise your authority in Christ by commanding sickness to leave. Speak His name and break any curses spoken over you. Use the power God gave you to shut up any lies the enemy may use against you. Stand firm on the Word of God.

_____

_____

_____

_____

_____

_____

_____

_____

_____

DAY 50

Be Loosed

But when Jesus saw her, He called her to Him and said to her, "Woman, you are loosed from your infirmity." And He laid His hands on her, and immediately she was made straight, and glorified God.

So ought not this woman, being a daughter of Abraham, whom Satan has bound—think of it—for eighteen years, be loosed from this bond on the Sabbath?"

—Luke 13:12, 16

This verse expresses that sickness is satanic bondage, and we ought to be loosed today of that bondage. God wants us to be free from the devil's works. Jesus came to destroy those works, and He has accomplished all that the Father sent Him

101

to do. He is seated at the right hand of God. Jesus came back to seek and save all who were lost. He came to heal the sick. There's no record anywhere that He made people sick. He only healed and loosed people from sickness and disease. He did the work and the will of the Father.

If you need healing or deliverance, receive it now in the name of Jesus. All sickness is broken in Jesus' name. Any evil spirit assigned to you has to leave.

Speak healing over yourself because of what Jesus accomplished on the cross. Declare the Words of the Father over yourself; be loosed and set free from bondage.

_____

_____

_____

_____

_____

_____

_____

_____

_____

DAY 51

The Bread of Life

*For the bread of God is He who comes down
from heaven and gives life to the world."*
—John 6:33

Jesus was the Word, and when He came to the earth, He had life in Him. He was the life of God, and He is the bread of life. We have the bread of life in us because we have Jesus. Jesus is life, and He is in us; therefore, we have life. The light that is in Jesus dispels darkness in our lives. He is the very image and representation of the Father. When you accepted Jesus, you received life, and His power is in you. The same power that rose Jesus from the dead lives in you (Romans 8:11). It is alive in you. His power is permeating your body and your mind. If you encounter weakness, sickness in your body, or any

103

type of demonic attack, receive healing right now. No devil in hell is going to come anywhere near the glory that's inside of you. Be healed!

> *In Him was life, and the life was the light of men.*
>
> —John 1:4

Today when you go into the marketplace, let your light shine and encourage someone who needs a touch of Jesus' life in them. Write about your day.

_____

_____

_____

_____

_____

_____

_____

_____

_____

_____

_____

DAY 52

Words of Life

It is the Spirit who gives life; the flesh profits nothing. The words that I speak to you are spirit, and they are life.

—John 6:63

Jesus' words are spirit, and they are life. When He walked the earth, He only said what the Father was saying. Those words were from the very throne of God. God spoke through Jesus, and He has given you the Spirit of God. He has given life to you through the Spirit. His words are like food and health for your body. God has spoken over you, and He sings songs of deliverance over you (Psalm 32:7). God is a warrior, and He loves you. His words are spirit, and they are alive. Receive the healing life of God!

The Lord your God in your midst, The Mighty One, will save; He will rejoice over you with gladness, He will quiet you with His love, He will rejoice over you with singing."
—Zephaniah 3:17 NIV

When you go out today, share the Words of Jesus with people. His Words produce life and healing. Write your experience of ministering to others.

_____

_____

_____

_____

_____

_____

_____

_____

_____

_____

_____

_____

DAY 53

Abundant Life

The thief does not come except to steal, and to kill, and to destroy. I have come that they may have life, and that they may have it more abundantly.

—John 10:10

J esus is on your side. He has already gone before you and destroyed your enemies. He has already spoken in favor of you to the Father. Jesus hung on a cross to spare you the torment of hell. Now that you are saved, allow Him to heal your body and expedite deliverance in your life. If anything is holding you back, such as addiction, doubtful thoughts, torment, or condemnation, you need to be delivered from it right now. Those things are not part of the abundant life. Jesus gave you abundant life. Overflowing power is working right now in the name of Jesus. He came to give life to you more abundantly.

Surrender anything that contradicts living in alignment with the abundant life. Jesus paid the price for it by dying on the cross. Give it all to Him, and receive His healing. Write about it here.

_____

_____

_____

_____

_____

_____

_____

_____

_____

_____

_____

_____

_____

_____

DAY 54

Resurrection Life

Jesus said to her, "I am the resurrection and the life. He who believes in Me, though he may die, he shall live.

—John 11:25

There is power in the resurrection of Jesus. He's seated at the right hand of God. He defeated the devil and won. You can ask anything in His name, and He's going to give it to you (John 14:14). His power is welling up within you right now.

Put a demand on the benefits that God has already given you. It's not so much a question of asking Him because He's already provided for you in advance to receive. God is with you in a mighty way, and His

109

resurrection is dwelling powerfully within you, causing your body to be well in the name of Jesus.

Ask Him for anything. Ask for your healing and deliverance. Whatever you need to see the Father do in your life, ask, and you shall receive.

_____

_____

_____

_____

_____

_____

_____

_____

_____

_____

_____

_____

_____

_____

DAY 55

Healed by Faith

And His name, through faith in His name, has made this man strong, whom you see and know. Yes, the faith which comes through Him has given him this perfect soundness in the presence of you all.

—Acts 3:16

The person in Acts 3:16 was made perfect and received complete healing by faith in Jesus' name. Faith in Jesus makes you strong and gives you perfect soundness. It was faith in the name of Jesus that healed him miraculously.

In another instance, Peter and John met a lame beggar and said, "Silver and gold have I none, But that which I have, I give unto you. In the name of

111

Jesus, get up and walk", and the man danced and leaped and received his healing (Acts 3:6-9). Peter and John healed the lame man. It was the name of Jesus and the faith that came through him that healed the man. You have access to the same healing. Whatever you're going through, it is by faith in the name of Jesus that you receive strength and soundness in your body. Receive it right now. Say the name of Jesus. It is a mighty name!

Pray with faith today for your healing. Your faith in Jesus produces strength and perfect soundness in your body. Write about what you encounter in prayer.

_____

_____

_____

_____

_____

_____

_____

_____

_____

DAY 56

The Word of God Heals

My son, give attention to my words; incline your ear to my sayings. Do not let them depart from your eyes; keep them in the midst of your heart; For they are life to those who find them, And health to all their flesh.
　　　　　　　　　　　　—Proverbs 4:20-22

The Lord wants to heal your mind and body today. He is telling you to meditate on His word and let it heal you. His words are medicine and health to your body. Solomon wrote this verse knowing that these words have healing in them and that they produce life to your flesh, because they came from God's mouth.

God sent Jesus to bring life and destroy the works of the devil. Jesus defeated the enemy and healed everyone who the devil oppressed. He wants to heal you. Any kind of hindrance or disease trying to afflict your body has to leave because Jesus defeated it. Every spiritual entity attacking you is broken and has to go. Trust in the Lord and let His name be glorified in your life.

Speak healing and life over yourself. Build yourself up with the faith that you are healed because God's Word says it. You have life flowing through you. Write about what you encounter.

_____

_____

_____

_____

_____

_____

_____

_____

DAY 57

A Good Report

*The light of the eyes rejoiceth the heart: and
a good report maketh the bones fat.*
——Proverbs 15:30 KJV

The Lord rewards those with a good report, and we see this throughout the whole Bible. When the spies returned from the Promised Land, they had received bad reports, but there were two, Joshua and Caleb, who had a good report, which caused them to live the next 40 years, and they got to see the Promised Land.

God is saying, "my good report makes your bones fat." He is speaking from His throne right now. Concentrate on what is coming from the mouth of God; rather than listening to all the bad reports you could be tuning into all day. He is the healer of all sickness and disease, and He wants to bring healing to the marrow in your bones. He is healing mental fatigue and mental fog in the name of Jesus. All aches and pains are leaving your joints right now in Jesus' name. Be encouraged and receive your healing right now!

Spend time hearing what the Lord is saying throughout the day. Follow His direction and be observant of how He interacts with you. Write down what you encountered with Him.

_____

_____

_____

_____

_____

_____

_____

_____

_____

_____

DAY 58

His Words are Health to your Body

Pleasant words are like a honeycomb, Sweetness to the soul, and health to the bones.

—Proverbs 16:24

Solomon wrote this verse in Proverbs, and he was a very wise man. He knew that God's Word is eternal. It is sweet to your soul and brings health to your bones. God never doubts what He says. When He sits on His throne and speaks, He waits for His Word to come back to Him; accomplishing exactly what He spoke it to be (Isaiah 55:11). He is speaking over you that you are well and healed. Expect His Word to be fulfilled. Remember what Paul said? The power that rose Jesus from the dead is dwelling in you, and it's quickening your mortal body (Romans 8:11).

If there is any type of healing you need in your body, receive it now from the Lord. Any pain or arthritis that you are experiencing is leaving you in Jesus' name. He is building up your immune system and strengthening you. God's Word is healing every part of you in the name of Jesus.

Meditate on today's scripture. Allow this word to go into the deeper places within. Let it become alive in you. Write about what you experience.

_____

_____

_____

_____

_____

_____

_____

_____

_____

_____

DAY 59

Joy comes from The Lord

Don't be dejected and sad, for the joy of the LORD is your strength!"
—Nehemiah 8:10 NLT

The joy coming from the Lord is your strength, and He is giving it to you. Joy is like medicine for your body. The joy of the Lord comes from Heaven. Joy is a spiritual characteristic of God. He is supplying it to you and giving you your strength back. Joy is like a medicine that you can take, and it comes from the supernatural realm, so make sure to take an extra dose of joy today. The Father is healing your body and breaking any mental torment, and healing brain fog. Receive your healing and receive the joy of the Lord.

Is there anything compromising your joy? A belief or a thought that's not aligned with God's word? Take it captive and invite His Word and joy to come and bring clarity. Write about any revelation you receive.

_____

_____

_____

_____

_____

_____

_____

_____

_____

_____

_____

_____

_____

_____

DAY 60

Healing in the Last Days

The eyes of those who see will not be dim,
And the ears of those who hear will listen.
—Isaiah 32:3

Isaiah prophesies that blind eyes will be opened. They will see and not be dim, and deaf ears will hear. In these end times, you are going to see more supernatural healing happening than ever before. We have seen many moves of God come to pass over the years. In this last day, God is moving by His spirit, and the Bible says that all people will experience the outpouring of the Spirit. The Spirit of God will be poured out on all flesh (Acts 2:17).

God's Word is here right now to remind you that healing is the children's bread. If you're having pain

121

in your body, you can believe for a miracle because of the truth of God's Word. Receive it now in the name of Jesus!

How can you align yourself and be ready for this move of God that's coming? How will you join in partnership with God to release healing to others?

_____

_____

_____

_____

_____

_____

_____

_____

_____

_____

_____

SALVATION PRAYER

Lord God,
I confess that I am a sinner.
I confess that I need Your Son, Jesus.
Please forgive me in His name.
Lord Jesus, I believe You died for me and that
You are alive and listening to me now.
I now turn from my sins and welcome You into my
heart. Come and take control of my life.
Make me the kind of person You want me to be.
Now, fill me with Your Holy Spirit, who will show me
how to live for You. I acknowledge You before men as
my Savior and my Lord. In Jesus' name. Amen.

If you prayed this prayer, please contact us at
info@kevinzadai.com for more information and
materials

We welcome you to join our network at
Warriornotes.tv for access to exclusive programming

To enroll in our ministry school, go to:
Warriornotesschool.com

Visit KevinZadai.com for additional ministry
materials

ABOUT DR. KEVIN L. ZADAI

Kevin Zadai, Th.D., was called to the ministry at the age of ten. He attended Central Bible College in Springfield, Missouri, where he received a bachelor of arts in theology. Later, he received training in missions at Rhema Bible College and a Th. D. at Primus University. He is currently ordained through Rev. Dr. Jesse and Rev. Dr. Cathy Duplantis.

At the age of thirty-one, during a routine day surgery, he found himself "on the other side of the veil" with Jesus. For forty-five minutes, the Master revealed spiritual truths before returning him to his body and assigning him to a supernatural ministry.

Kevin holds a commercial pilot license and is retired from Southwest Airlines after twenty-nine years as a flight attendant. Kevin is the founder and president of Warrior Notes School of Ministry. He and his lovely wife, Kathi, reside in New Orleans, Louisiana.

Other Books and Study Guides
By Dr. Kevin L. Zadai

*Kevin has written over fifty books and study guides
Please see our website at www.Kevinzadai.com for
a complete list of materials!*

*A Meeting Place with God,
The Heavenly Encounters
Series Volume 1*

*The Heavenly Encounters
Series Volume 1*

The Agenda of Angels

*The Agenda of Angels
Study Guide*

Days of Heaven on Earth

*Days of Heaven on Earth:
A Study Guide to the Days
Ahead*

*Days of Heaven on Earth
Prayer and Confession
Guide*

*Encountering the Heavenly
Sapphire Devotional*

*Encountering the Heavenly
Sapphire Study Guide:*

Encountering God's Will

*Encountering God's
Normal Study Guide*

*From Breakthrough to
Overthrow Study Guide*

*Have you Been to
the Altar Lately?*

Heavenly Visitation

*Heavenly Visitation: A
Study Guide to
Participating in the
Supernatural*

*Heavenly Visitation
Prayer and Confession
Guide*

128

*Your Hidden Destiny
Revealed, The Heavenly
Encounters Series Volume 2*

*Praying From the Heavenly
Realms Study Guide*

*Warrior Fellowships
Season 1
Volume 1 Study Guide*

*Warrior Fellowships
Season 1
Volume 2 Study Guide*

*Warrior Notes Aviation
Volume 1: Flight Manual
Study Guide*

*Warrior Women
Volume 1 Study Guide
Warrior Women
Volume 2 Study Guide*

*Warrior Justice: A Study
Guide to Experiencing
Freedom from Demonic
Oppression*

Made in the USA
Coppell, TX
27 September 2021